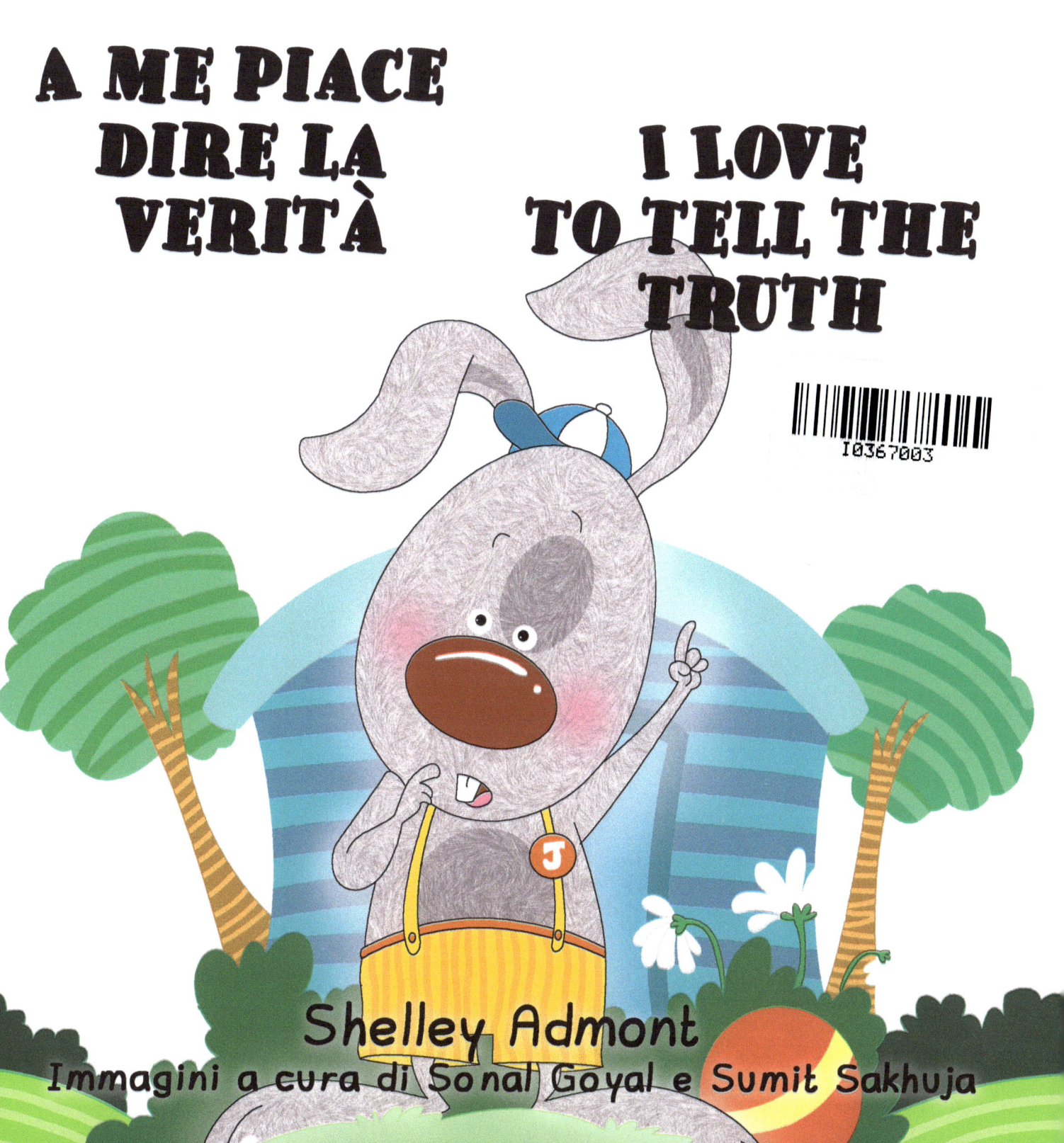

www.kidkiddos.com
Copyright©2015 by S.A.Publishing ©2017 by KidKiddos Books Ltd.
support@kidkiddos.com

All rights reserved. No part of this book may be reproduced in any form or by any electronic or mechanical means, including information storage and retrieval systems, without written permission from the publisher or author, except in the case of a reviewer, who may quote brief passages embodied in critical articles or in a review.

Tutti i diritti sono riservati. Nessuna parte di questa pubblicazione può essere riprodotta, memorizzata in sistemi di recupero o trasmessa in qualsiasi forma o attraverso qualsiasi mezzo elettronico, meccanico, mediante fotocopiatura, registrazione o altro, senza l'autorizzazione del possessore del copyright.
Second edition, 2019
Translated from English by Lucrezia Bertolino
Traduzione dall'inglese a cura di Lucrezia Bertolino

Library and Archives Canada Cataloguing in Publication
I Love to Tell the Truth (Italian English Bilingual Edition)/ Shelley Admont
ISBN: 978-1-5259-1187-3 paperback
ISBN: 978-1-77268-607-4 hardcover
ISBN: 978-1-77268-256-4 eBook

Please note that the Italian and English versions of the story have been written to be as close as possible. However, in some cases they differ in order to accommodate nuances and fluidity of each language.
Although the author and the publisher have made every effort to ensure the accuracy and completeness of information contained in this book, we assume no responsibility for errors, inaccuracies, omission, inconsistency, or consequences from such information.

Per quelli che amo di più–S.A.
For those I love the most–S.A.

Era una bellissima giornata d'estate. Il sole splendeva nel cielo. Gli uccellini cinguettavano. Le api e le farfalle svolazzavano tra i fiori colorati.

It was a beautiful summer day. The sun was shining brightly. The birds were chirping. The butterflies and the bees were busy visiting the colorful flowers.

Il coniglietto Jimmy stava giocando a palla in giardino con i suoi due fratelli più gradi. La loro mamma stava innaffiando le sue margherite preferite.

Little bunny Jimmy was playing ball in the backyard with his two older brothers. Their mom was watering her favorite daisies.

*"Attenti a non avvicinarvi ai miei fiori, bambini"
disse la mamma.*
"Be careful not to go near my flowers, boys,"
said mom.

"Certo mamma" gridò Jimmy.
"Sure mom," yelled Jimmy.

*"Non toccherò le tue margherite, mamma"
aggiunse il fratello di mezzo.*
"I won't touch your daises mom," added the
middle brother.

*"Non preoccuparti, mamma" disse il fratello
maggiore. "Le tue margherite sono al sicuro
con noi".*
"Don't worry mom," said the oldest brother.
"Your daisies are safe with us."

La mamma rientrò in casa, mentre i fratelli continuarono a giocare fuori, lanciandosi la palla tra loro.
Mom went back to the house while the brothers continued to play outside, tossing the ball to each other.

"Ehi, facciamo un altro gioco adesso" disse il fratello maggiore, facendo roteare la palla.
"Hey, let's play a different game now," said the oldest brother, twisting the ball.

"Che gioco?" chiese Jimmy.
"What game?" asked Jimmy.

Il fratello maggiore ci pensò per un secondo. "Lanciamo la palla in aria e vediamo chi la prende per primo" disse.
The oldest brother thought for a second. "Let's toss the ball in the air and see who gets to catch it first," he said.

"Mi piace!" disse Jimmy allegramente.
"I like that," said Jimmy cheerfully.

"Cominciamo" strillò il mezzano. "Lancia la palla adesso".

"Let's start," cried the middle brother. "Throw the ball now."

Il fratello maggiore lanciò la palla in aria più forte che poteva.

The oldest brother threw the ball up in the air as hard as he could.

Tutti i coniglietti alzarono la testa e osservarono a bocca aperta la grande palla arancione volare velocemente su nel cielo. Presto iniziò a scendere di nuovo verso terra.

All the bunnies looked up with their mouths open as the big orange ball quickly flew up. Soon, it began to fall back towards the ground.

I fratellini aspettarono impazienti allungando le loro mani.

Stretching out their hands, the brothers waited eagerly.

Proprio prima che la palla toccasse il suolo, i due fratelli più grandi corsero a prenderla.

When the ball was about to hit the ground, the older brothers ran to catch it.

In un attimo, Jimmy balzò in avanti e raggiunse la palla prima di loro. "Urrà! Ho vinto!"

In a flash, Jimmy leapt forward and reached the ball before them. "Hurray! I win!"

Fece dei salti di gioia e si mise a correre eccitato per tutto il giardino.

He jumped in joy and started to run around the backyard in excitement.

Improvvisamente, inciampò in una piccola roccia e finì lungo disteso per terra... proprio nel bel mezzo del cespuglio di margherite preferite della mamma.

Suddenly, he tripped over a small rock and fell flat on the ground ... right in the middle of his mom's favorite daisy plants.

"Ahia!" urlò Jimmy, alzando la testa dal terriccio bagnato.

"Ouch!" yelled Jimmy, lifting his head out of the wet soil.

Suo fratello maggiore gli corse incontro e lo aiutò a rimettersi in piedi. "Jimmy, ti sei fatto male?" gli chiese.

His oldest brother ran over and helped him back to his feet. "Jimmy, are you hurt?" he asked.

"No... Credo... di stare bene" disse Jimmy.

"No... I think I'm fine," said Jimmy.

I tre coniglietti guardarono tristi i fiori preferiti della loro mamma, che erano ormai tutti schiacciati. Alcuni si erano anche spezzati.

All three bunnies looked sadly at their mom's favourite yellow flowers, which were now crushed. Some of them were broken.

"Alla mamma questo proprio non piacerà" mormorò silenziosamente il fratello maggiore.

"Mom will not be happy to see this," murmured the oldest brother quietly.

"Sicuramente" concordò il fratello di mezzo.

"That's for sure," agreed the middle brother.

"Per favore, vi prego, non dite alla mamma che sono stato io. Vi preeeeego..." implorò Jimmy, allontanandosi lentamente dalle margherite rovinate.

"Please, please, don't tell mom that I did this. Pleeeeeaaaase..." begged Jimmy, slowly moving away from the ruined daisies.

In quel momento, la mamma uscì correndo di casa. "Bambini, cos'è successo? Ho appena sentito qualcuno gridare. State tutti bene?"

That moment, their mom came running out from the house. "Kids, what happened? I just heard someone scream. Are you all OK?"

"Noi sì, mamma" disse il fratello maggiore. "Ma i tuoi fiori..."

"We're fine, mom" said the oldest brother. "But your flowers..."

Fu solo in quel momento che la mamma notò l'aiuola distrutta. Sospirò. "Com'è successo?" chiese incredula.

It wasn't until that moment that their mom noticed the ruined flowerbed. She sighed. "How did this happen?" she asked, her shoulders drooping.

"Sono stati gli alieni" rispose esitando Jimmy. "Sono venuti da.... là fuori..." disse indicando il cielo. "Sul serio, mamma".
"It was aliens," Jimmy hastened to answer. "They came from... out there..." He pointed to the sky. "Really, mom."

La mamma alzò un sopracciglio e guardò Jimmy negli occhi. "Alieni?"
Mom raised her eyebrow and looked into Jimmy's eyes. "Aliens?"

"Sì, e sono volati via con la loro astronave".
"Yes, and they flew away in their spaceship."

La mamma sospirò di nuovo. "Meno male che sono volati via," disse, "perchè è ora di cena. Non dimenticate di lavarvi le mani. E tu, Jimmy..."
Mom sighed again. "It's good that they flew away," she said, "because now it's time for dinner. Don't forget to wash your hands. And Jimmy..."

"Sì, mamma" disse Jimmy.
"Yes, mom," said Jimmy.

"Và a lavarti anche la faccia" aggiunse.
"Go wash your face too," she added.

A cena, Jimmy era molto silenzioso. Si sentiva strano. Non riusciva a mangiare e non riusciva a bere. Non volle nemmeno assaggiare un pezzetto della sua torta di carote preferita.

During the dinner, Jimmy was very quiet. He felt uncomfortable. He couldn't eat and he couldn't drink. He didn't even want to try his favourite carrot cake.

Durante la notte, Jimmy non riuscì a dormire. Qualcosa non andava. Alzandosi, si avvicinò al letto di suo fratello maggiore.
At night, Jimmy couldn't sleep. Something didn't feel right. Getting up, he approached his oldest brother's bed.

"Hey, stai dormendo?" sussurrò.
"Hey, are you sleeping?" he whispered.

"Jimmy, che succede?" borbottò suo fratello maggiore, aprendo pian piano gli occhietti addormentati. "Torna nel tuo letto".
"Jimmy, what happened?" mumbled his oldest brother, slowly opening his sleepy eyes. "Go back to your bed."

"Non riesco a dormire. Continuo a pensare ai fiori di mamma" disse piano Jimmy. "Avrei dovuto fare più attenzione con loro".
"I can't sleep. I keep thinking about mom's flowers," said Jimmy quietly. "I should have been careful with them."

"Oh, ma è stato un incidente" disse il fratello più grande. "Non ti preoccupare. Torna a dormire!"
"Oh, that was an accident," said the oldest brother. "Don't worry. Go back to sleep!"

"Però non avrei dovuto mentire alla mamma" disse Jimmy, rimanendo ancora lì.
"But I should not have lied to mom," said Jimmy still staying there.

Suo fratello maggiore si mise a sedere sul letto. "Sì" concordò "Avresti dovuto dirle la verità".
The oldest brother sat up on his bed. "Yes," he agreed. "You should have told her the truth."

"Lo so" disse Jimmy, stringendosi nelle spalle. "E ora che faccio?"
"I know," said Jimmy, shrugging his shoulders. "What am I going to do now?"

"Per adesso, vai a dormire. E poi, domani mattina, dirai a mamma la verità. D'accordo?"
"For now, go to sleep. And in the morning, you will tell mom the truth. Deal?"

"OK" disse Jimmy e si trascinò lentamente a letto.

"OK," said Jimmy and he trudged slowly to his bed.

Il mattino dopo, si svegliò molto presto, saltò fuori dal letto e si affrettò a cercare la sua mamma. La trovò in giardino.

The next morning, he woke up very early, jumped out of his bed, and ran looking for his mom. She was in the backyard.

"Mamma" chiamò Jimmy. "Sono stato io a rovinare i tuoi fiori, non gli alieni." Le corse incontro e la abbracciò.

"Mommy," Jimmy called. "I was the one who ruined your flowers, not the aliens." He ran over and hugged his mom.

La mamma ricambiò il suo abbraccio e rispose "Sono così contenta che tu mi abbia detto la verità. So che non è stato facile, ma sono davvero fiera di te, Jimmy".

Mom hugged him back and replied, "I'm so happy that you told the truth. I know it wasn't easy, and I'm proud of you, Jimmy."

"Per favore, non essere triste per i fiori. Penseremo a qualcosa" disse Jimmy.

"Please don't be sad about the flowers. We'll think of something," said Jimmy.

La mamma scosse la testa. "Non ero preoccupata per i fiori. Ero triste perchè mi stavi tenendo nascosta la verità".

Mom shook her head. "I was not worried about the flowers. I was sad about you not telling me the truth."

"Mi dispiace, mamma" disse Jimmy. "Anch'io ero triste. Non dirò più bugie".

"I'm sorry, mom," said Jimmy. "I was sad also. I won't lie again."

Dopo colazione, Jimmy ed il suo papà andarono insieme al vivaio della città. Comprarono alcuni semi di margherita e tutta la famiglia aiutò la mamma a piantarli.

After breakfast, Jimmy visited the local plant nursery with his dad. They bought some daisy seedlings and the whole family helped mom plant them.

Jimmy ha imparato che dire la verità è ciò che rende lui e la sua famiglia felici. Ecco perché, da quel giorno in poi, dice sempre la verità.

Jimmy learned that telling the truth makes him and his family happy. That's why from that day on, he always tells the truth.

www.ingramcontent.com/pod-product-compliance
Lightning Source LLC
Chambersburg PA
CBHW061132070526
44584CB00033B/4298